adventures in **Sand**

David M. Baird

inside this book

1. sand adventures

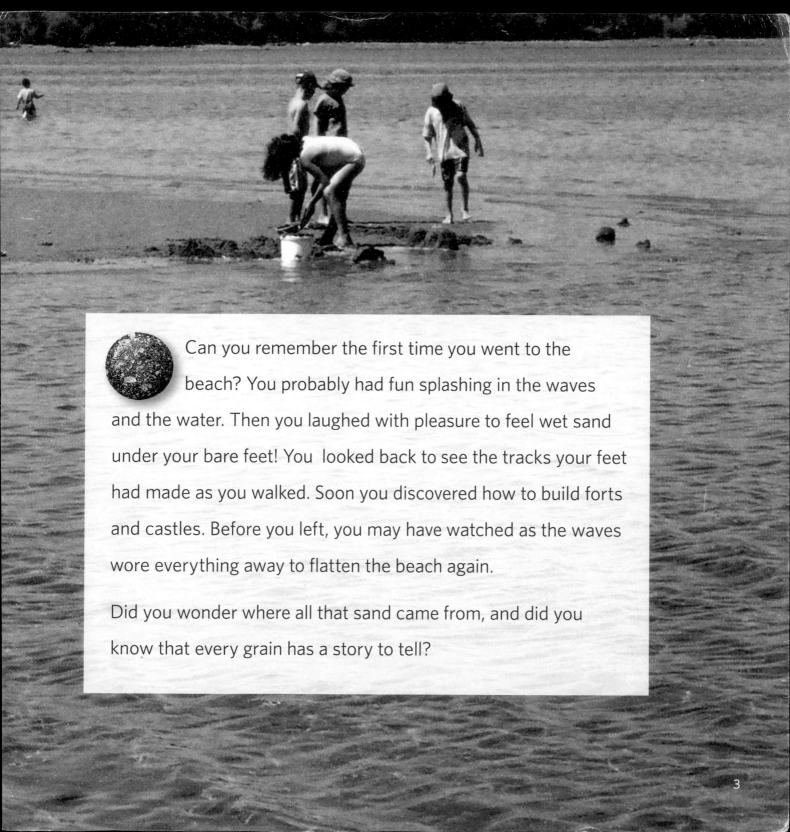

Can you remember the first time you went to the beach? You probably had fun splashing in the waves and the water. Then you laughed with pleasure to feel wet sand under your bare feet! You looked back to see the tracks your feet had made as you walked. Soon you discovered how to build forts and castles. Before you left, you may have watched as the waves wore everything away to flatten the beach again.

Did you wonder where all that sand came from, and did you know that every grain has a story to tell?

a first glimpse of adventures

Shell sand

You could get a first glimpse into the adventures that lurk in sand by picking up a handful of it the next time you get a chance. Look at it up close and you will probably see several different kinds of grains. They may be dark or light, smooth or rough, glassy or dull, flat or round, and almost any colour. They may all be rock fragments or bits of pure minerals or bits of different coloured shells. Mostly they are mixtures of all these.

Dark beach sand with dark lava fragments and slatey rocks and a few shell fragments and light minerals

Buff beach sand – mostly clear quartz and yellowish shell fragments with a few bits of dark rock

sand!
everywhere sand!

A winding river in Ontario shows sand and gravel bars on the insides of bends.

Beaches and the shores of lakes are not the only places to find sand. Most rivers and streams have sand bars and beaches too. Where they empty into the sea, they deposit silt and sand in their deltas. You know from pictures that sand dunes are features of deserts all over the world. You can also see them at the backs of most windy beaches. Sand grains are even hidden in most soils. Indeed, some plants such as peach trees and rhubarb require especially sandy soils.

Mountain climbers find small pockets of frost-riven sand collecting in crevices at great heights. Sand grains are found in muds of the deep sea because desert windstorms waft sand grains out over adjacent oceans. Sand seems to be everywhere!

Beach and dunes, Sand Dunes Provincial Park, Ontario

Clear quartz grains mixed with bits of pink granite and a few shell fragments

5

it's **useful** stuff

Sand occurs almost everywhere naturally, and people all over the world have used it in hundreds of ways. For thousands of years, people have strengthened bricks by adding a little sand to the clay before baking them. You've probably seen sand being thrown onto sidewalks and roads to make them less slippery in winter. Construction workers use it to make concrete for foundations and walls. It's a big part of plaster and mortar for brickwork and masonry.

People use millions of bags of sand to keep back floods in spring. Sharp sand is put into powerful jets of air to blast and clean grimy old buildings and rusty ships in drydock. It's used to make abrasive sandpaper for polishing wood and metal. In winter, a layer of sand adds friction to icy railway tracks.

Concrete barriers and asphalt are mostly sand and fine gravel.

Did you know that the eyeglasses that some of you wear start as pure quartz sand? And so does the glass in jam jars and windows, the fronts of television sets, and beautiful vases. For thousands of years, people have made walls and buildings from sandstone found in old sand deposits that have solidified into stone. Prospectors go countless miles through rough country to pan for gold on sand bars in remote streams. Tourists travel all over the world to walk and sun themselves on warm sandy beaches.

Almost all glass starts as pure sand.

When you drive on modern highways, sand is a major ingredient of the concrete or asphalt surface. On golf courses, nice white sand is brought from afar to make the bunkers and traps that golfers want to avoid. Old iron frying pans, and maybe even parts of heavy old iron stoves themselves, were cast in special moulding sand. The drinking water you had today was probably filtered through beds of sand to purify it.

Sand is certainly useful stuff!

The lenses in this old camera started as pure quartz sand from the coast of Europe.

Southern Ontario red sandstone

Ottawa area sandstone

The old library, Parliament buildings, Ottawa

Fine sand

Coarse sand

Pebbles

Smaller cobbles

cobbles

Ovoid cobble

2. just what is sand?

Experts have to be exact in what they say so they describe sand as particles of rocks, minerals or shells between 0.05 mm and 2.0 mm across. That means that sand grains are roughly the same size as grains of salt, coarse brown sugar or mustard seed. Silt and dust are even smaller. Larger bits are called pebbles, cobbles and boulders.

For comparison the smallest ones are the same size as the tiny particles in flour and icing sugar. Pebbles range in size from small peas up to golf balls. Cobbles range from golf-ball size to the size of bowling balls or small pumpkins. Boulders range in size from pumpkins all the way up to small houses. On your next trip to the beach, see how many different sizes of particles you can find.

Waves wash this large boulder and cobbles left on a Newfoundland shore by the ice sheet that once covered most of Canada.

So many **colours** and **kinds**

You have probably noticed already that there are lots of kinds and colours of sand. You might have guessed that this is because different kinds of sand come from different sources. How many different colours have you seen? If grains of sand can have so many different colours and origins, let's find out more about them. In the meantime, is it any wonder that people collect samples of sand to remind themselves of wonderful places they have been!

dark sand in collector's bottle

Sand samples from all over the world on glass study slides

9

An artificial sand of highly angular grains was made by grinding up feldspar crystals.

frosting, rounding and **shapes**

The shapes of sand grains have an important effect on how they look and feel. As they are moved in wind or water currents, they bang against one another and against bottom rocks. Big ones roll onto smaller ones and break them. These processes round off the corners. How round the sand grain is shows how much it has travelled or how rough a time it has had.

Water-carried grains are smoother than wind-carried grains, which tend to be frosted looking. This is because particles can hit one another more easily in air than in water, which supplies a cushioning effect.

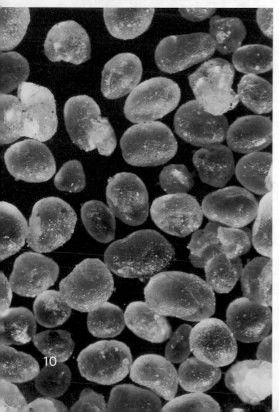

Much-rounded grains are from a natural quartz sand that has undergone long transportation and wearing in wind and water.

The bits worn off the original blocks to make these rounded boulders in a wall are now sand somewhere far away.

"Rounding" just refers to the corners being smoothed off. When particles break off rocks they are apt to be angular and sharp edged. They can be more or less cubic, elongated, flat and disc shaped, or skinny and stick-like. Rounding leads to shapes that are described as spheroid (perfectly round as a golf ball); discoid or lenticular (like lenses in a magnifying glass or eyeglasses); or round-edged sticks (like "cheesies" or stubby pencils).

Look among the rocks. How many shapes can you find?

3. how sand is made

The light-coloured sand dunes in most deserts are made of grains of the mineral quartz from decayed rocks. So are many of the dazzling white beaches of eastern Australia, the Gulf of Mexico, and the Atlantic coast of the United States. The pink sands of Bermuda and the white beaches of the Bahamas are made of bits of broken coral or other shells. Pockets of green sands in Newfoundland and Nova Scotia come from the green sea urchins that grow there. Beaches of black sand are features in Iceland, Hawaii, Indonesia and other volcanic areas. The world-famous reddish sands of Prince Edward Island come from eroding cliffs of reddish sandstone nearby.

When you held a handful of sand up close and saw the separate grains, you saw that they are simply tiny pieces of broken rock, minerals or shells. And seeing so many different kinds of sand, you guessed that they must start in different ways. So to see where sand comes from, we should look to places where rocks and shells are being broken down and see how the fragments are being collected together to make sandbars, beaches and dunes.

Red Deer River, born in the Rockies, drops part of its huge load of sand and gravel as the current slows down where it meets the plains in western Alberta.

wave action and running water

Did you ever think that you can actually watch and hear new sand being made along shorelines? In times of storm with big waves, people on shore can actually hear the crashing of boulders against one another and against the rocky cliffs. The rumble of moving stones is particularly noticeable in the back-wash of large waves. Fragments of rock are broken off, and they in turn get worn down. This is the beginning of one kind of sand.

Another place to look is where swiftly flowing rivers and streams push rocks of all sizes against one another and along river bottoms. This produces new sand. Running water also collects particles produced by weathering, frost action, glacial action and other processes. This is the way large deposits in sand bars, beaches and deltas are made.

Curving spits on Nova Scotia's south coast were made by waves carrying sand and gravel along the shore from different directions.

See how storm waves have gone over the top on the this beach making little points on the back.

Tide mark

sand from **glaciers**

You probably know that in the last million years or so, an enormous sheet of glacial ice covered the northern half of North America, including almost all of Canada and some of the northern United States. The ice disappeared in a climate-warming cycle only about 10,000 to 20,000 years ago. The massive ice scraped away everything as it moved over the countryside. It also ground into the solid rocks below, plucking and scratching, making new sand.

Cliffs of water-washed glacial sands make a new beach below.

When the great glacier was melting, gushing meltwaters picked up boulders, cobbles, sand grains and ground-up rock. All these were deposited in distinctive bars, mounds and hills. In some places, sand grains were winnowed out and then re-deposited by the running meltwater. From these deposits, we can now extract well-washed sand and gravel. Beaches on most Canadian lakes, rivers and sea coasts are made of these glacial deposits that are being reworked by waves and currents. This is happening sometimes even as we watch.

Front of a present-day glacier in the Canadian Arctic with gushing meltwater and glacial debris, including new sand

wind wears away solid rocks

How would wind wear away rock? If you stand on a sandy beach or a sand dune in a strong wind, you can feel the sting of wind-carried sand grains on your skin. Over time, wind borne sand can wear away solid rock to make new sand. Wind borne sand is especially active in regions where old sandstones are exposed. In places where long droughts have dried out the soil, wind may pick up sand particles to make dunes. In some deserts, salts are left behind when temporary lakes dry up. Wind may then pick up the dried white crystals and deposit them else-where. This is the origin of dazzling white dunes in New Mexico.

Ripples on a sand dune at Cape Hatteras, US

Note how the lighter grains are concentrated on the crests of the ripples.

Wind- and sand-eroded sandstones, the Milk River valley, Alberta

mechanical abrasion and sand

Can you imagine rocks breaking and smashing into smaller bits as they fall off cliffs in the mountains? A lot of grinding and breaking also goes on in landslides and avalanches. Earthquakes and other large-scale earth movements make more sand by causing mechanical breakage of rocks.

At Mt. Columbia, Jasper National Park, new sand is made by rocks crashing down from the cliffs.

A ship with horses was wrecked on Sable Island off the coast of Nova Scotia a couple of hundred years ago. Two descendants are running here along the beautiful quartz sand beach in the pure joy of living.

Coarse, nearly pure quartz sand from Sable Island

sand from rocks decaying in the weather

The most common sand grains are made of quartz, a white or glassy mineral made of silicon and oxygen. When molten magma, cools and crystallizes deep in the earth, it may form granite. Granite is made of interlocking grains of quartz (glassy, clear or white), feldspar (pink, yellowish or white), and mica or other dark minerals such as hornblende or magnetite.

These minerals all figure in the story of sand because erosion has exposed large areas of granite on the surface of the earth. In ordinary surface weathering, all but the quartz grains decay slowly. Running water and wind can then pick up the loosened quartz grains and some of the others to concentrate them as sand in beaches, sandbanks or dunes.

Polished granite shows reddish, yellow and white feldspars and glassy quartz in interlocking crystals.

sand from **shells**

Waves dislodge shells and pick up abandoned ones in places where the sea is full of shelled creatures. These are mostly corals, snails, mussels, clams and urchins. Waves and currents then grind the shells up and deposit them to form sand beaches. Some of these shell sands are so coarse that you can still identify bits and pieces of the original shells. When the bits get finely ground, they become sand grains, mostly white but sometimes pink or green or blue.

Beach coquina, a sand being made of fragmented shells, Vancouver Island

Sand made mostly of round shells of tiny foraminifera, Bali, Indonesia

sand from **volcanoes**

The dark clouds of roiling smoke coming out of erupting volcanoes are sometimes filled with droplets of very hot, liquid lava. When these cool, solidify and fall to the ground, they become sand grains. In some violent eruptions, dense clouds of smoke full of chunks of lava mixed with steam and hot volcanic gasses rush down the steep sides of volcanoes. Can you imagine the violent crashing, grinding and pulverizing of everything inside them?

Red-hot lavas hitting cool seawater may shatter into tiny fragments. Black sands that began this way are common on the beaches of Hawaii, the Caribbean Islands and most other volcanic regions of the world.

Mixed dark lava and shell sand, James Island, Galapagos →

Lots of volcanic sand being formed right now on the active volcano, Anik Krakatoa, Indonesia

second-hand sands

Large deposits of sand may solidify over a long time to form sandstone. In most of these sandstones, the original grains, though tightly bound together, are still recognizable. If wind, waves or running water wear away sandstone ledges, the original grains may be released and once again become active sand. Thus we have a second-generation sand. Many famous Australian beaches lie below eroding sandstone cliffs and are made this way.

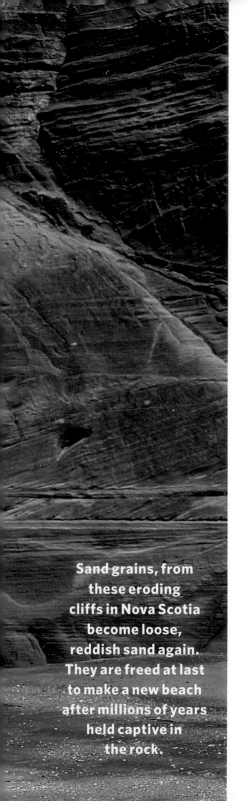

Sand grains, from these eroding cliffs in Nova Scotia become loose, reddish sand again. They are freed at last to make a new beach after millions of years held captive in the rock.

how long does it take to make a beach, a dune, or a mountain?

From earliest times, some people have wondered about how long it takes to build mountains, carve river valleys or build dunes and beaches. They could see that some geological processes are very fast. You might think of earthquakes, volcanic eruptions and landslides. These take only a few minutes to make large changes in the landscape. But others are very slow and go on for vast periods of time.

Mt. Sir Donald, B.C.

Nowadays scientists use the regular ticking of radioactive elements to give accurate measurements of the earth's history. The oldest rocks we know of are more than 4,000 million years old! Some of these ancient rocks are in northern Canada. Almost all young people know that dinosaurs roamed the earth part way along this time span, until they died out about 65 million years ago.

All this means that the earth has had lots of time to make large deposits of sand, even at one grain at a time. We also know from studying the record in the rocks that sands have been part of the scene since ancient volcanoes belched out clouds of ash and the first rains began to fall on the land billions of years ago.

4. ancient stories in sand

Sandstones in Utah were sand dunes in an ancient desert millions of years ago.

Note the visible dune-type cross-bedding structures.

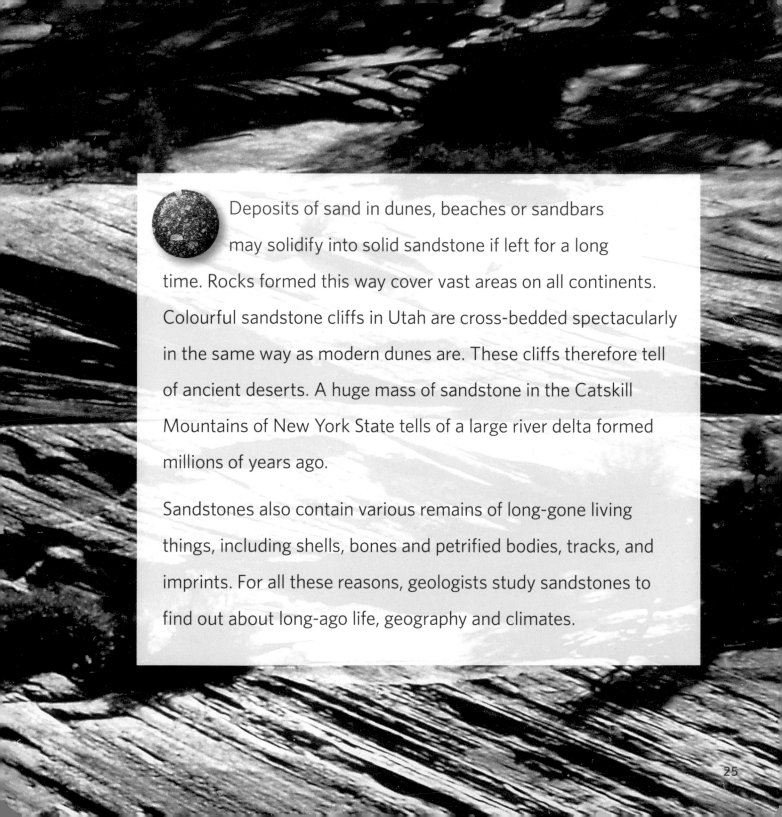

Deposits of sand in dunes, beaches or sandbars may solidify into solid sandstone if left for a long time. Rocks formed this way cover vast areas on all continents. Colourful sandstone cliffs in Utah are cross-bedded spectacularly in the same way as modern dunes are. These cliffs therefore tell of ancient deserts. A huge mass of sandstone in the Catskill Mountains of New York State tells of a large river delta formed millions of years ago.

Sandstones also contain various remains of long-gone living things, including shells, bones and petrified bodies, tracks, and imprints. For all these reasons, geologists study sandstones to find out about long-ago life, geography and climates.

scientists and a handful of sand

Now you can see why some scientists spend their whole lives studying sand and sandstone. When you understand how sand is made, you know how scientists can use sandstones to read stories of Earth's history. Fossil remains tell of ancient life. In the sandy rocks themselves, scientists see records of ancient mountains rising and eroding, of changing seashores, of deserts and deltas long disappeared, and even of ancient undersea landslides.

Scientists travel all over the world to squat on sea beaches, on sandbars in rivers, on sand dunes in deserts and on outcrops of sandstone. There they examine the sand and sandstone records closely. They go on to write books and learned articles and solemnly give lectures on their findings.

Several sets of dinosaur tracks on an ancient river bar in northern Alberta. Which way were they walking?

A dinosaur on a sandy flat beside an ancient sea millions of years ago

you can walk where dinosaurs walked

Some rock surfaces in western Canada, Nova Scotia, Utah and the Gobi Desert show dinosaur footprints. Some rocks contain bones, and sometimes whole skeletons. The rocks themselves tell what it was like when dinosaurs roamed along the muddy sandbars beside old rivers and along the edges of long-disappeared seas. In places like these, you can actually walk where dinosaurs walked millions of years before you came along.

5. more sand adventures

Wave ripples at low tide on
a beach on the west coast of
Newfoundland

You can share in the scientists' adventures in sand at the edge of the water where waves are coming in. Every wave picks up some of the sand and carries it forward up the beach. As the water recedes, it carries the sand back down again. During a storm, the upward movement is much stronger, and the beach builds up more steeply. If the waves are coming in at an angle to the shoreline, the sweep of the waves carries sand grains along the beach. A sure proof of this is the way sand collects on one side or the other of rocky points, wharves, breakwaters, or even driftwood logs and occasional boulders.

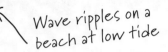
Wave ripples on a beach at low tide

watch **ripples** forming

Most beaches, sand bars and dunes are ripple marked by waves, currrents and wind. If the tide goes out gently on rippled sea beaches, the ripple marks may be left exposed in perfect condition. This lets you admire first hand the limitless variety of symmetrical patterns. Even better – if you wade out in shallow water with waves coming in over a sandy bottom, you can actually watch the ripples being formed. See how some of the grains are moving more actively than others. These are almost always the lighter coloured or smaller ones because they are lighter in weight than the darker or larger grains. These last sometimes get left behind to form dark streaks and patterns.

Sand grains on the surfaces of dunes are also in constant motion, and you can watch the individual grains being trundled along by the wind. Again you can see ripples being formed. You may also note that the grains on the crests of the ripples are smaller and lighter than those in the troughs.

Rill

30

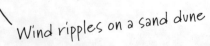
Wind ripples on a sand dune

rills and tracks

As the tide goes out on ocean beaches, trapped water oozes out of the sand just uncovered. It may form little streams called rills. These sometimes look like miniatures of real river systems seen from airplane windows. You can also see bird tracks, snail and worm trails, and clam holes.

Rill

Mottling on a beach made by waves separating the heavier and darker particles and carrying away the lighter ones

Seabird tracks

Rill

Rill

Swash
marks

Swash
marks

look for **swash marks**

Stoop down and look at the beach where the waves are coming in. Look especially closely at the place where the very top of each wave reaches before the water recedes. You will almost always see lines of lighter fragments left behind there – tiny bits of wood , darker seaweed or lighter minerals such as mica flakes, and the like. These lines are called "swash marks," a lovely word that sounds like the breaking waves that make the marks.

sand **sorting**

Sand begins in a jumble of rocks, from dust size to boulders, under eroding cliffs at the seashore, in debris below mountains, or under moving glaciers. Sorting begins as soon as running water or wind gets at it. Smaller bits or ones made of lighter minerals are the first to be carried away. Later, when these are deposited in bars, beaches and dunes, sands of a particular kind are accumulated. This is why sandy beaches occur below eroding cliffs of mixed glacial debris. Dunes of beautifully sorted fine sand are often seen at the backs of windy beaches.

After rocks are ground up or decay in the weather, some of the mineral grains may become concentrated. Sands rich in gold, zircon, tin minerals, magnetite or even gem stones are made this way. Because quartz is very common and the most resistant of minerals, it becomes the most common sand.

Almost all our northern beaches have places where waves have sorted out lines and pockets of black magnetite (a common iron mineral) or reddish garnet clearly visible against the lighter common sand.

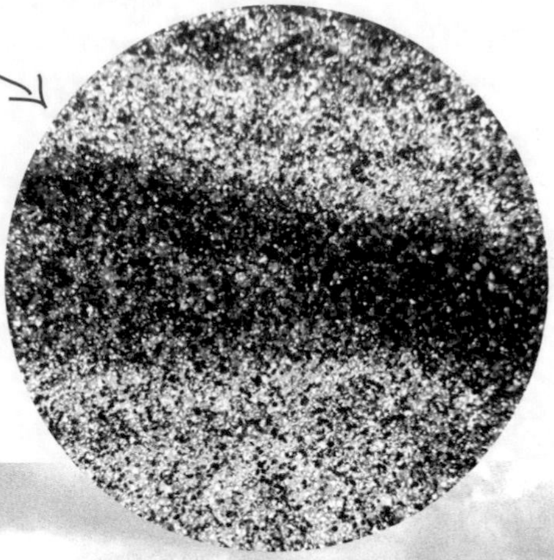

light quartz sand

dark garnet sand

Erosion of the red cliff supplied boulders just below it.

The sand winnowed out from the boulders has been carried to the zoned beach.

33

pores in **sand, oil,** and drinking **water**

Most oil deposits occur in the pores of sandstones or limestones, where they have accumulated over the ages. For this reason, geologists pay a lot of attention to sandstones, and especially porous ones, when they are searching for oil and gas. Oil deposits are often thousands of metres underground, and can be reached only by deep drilling, often followed by pumping the oil.

Porous sandstones underground may also supply the well water that makes it possible to live in dry areas. These areas may even be semi-deserts as in the southwestern United States and Australia. The underground water in the sandstone pores actually comes from rain soaking down from the surface. That may happen right there or far away where the same porous rock formations actually poke up to the surface.

Oil well pump
and gas flare

34

find the **pore** space

Look at any pile of pebbles or cobbles on the beach and you will see lots of empty spaces between them because they don't fit together very well. But did you know that this "pore" space can be as much as one-third of the total volume in a bag of golf balls or a can of peas or a pail of sand?

If you are curious about this, you can do an experiment the next time you are at the beach. First, fill a can or other container with clean cobbles and pebbles one to three centimetres across until the bucket is "full." Next, get another container and fill it with very dry sand. Now pour the dry sand on top of the pebbles and watch it disappear into the pore spaces in the "full" load of pebbles.

You can go one step more after the container is "full" of sand and pebbles. Add water to the mixture and watch it disappear into the remaining pore spaces. This proves that a lot of the contents of a seemingly full container can be pore space.

The space between pebbles seems to be full.

Here the light shows the pore space.

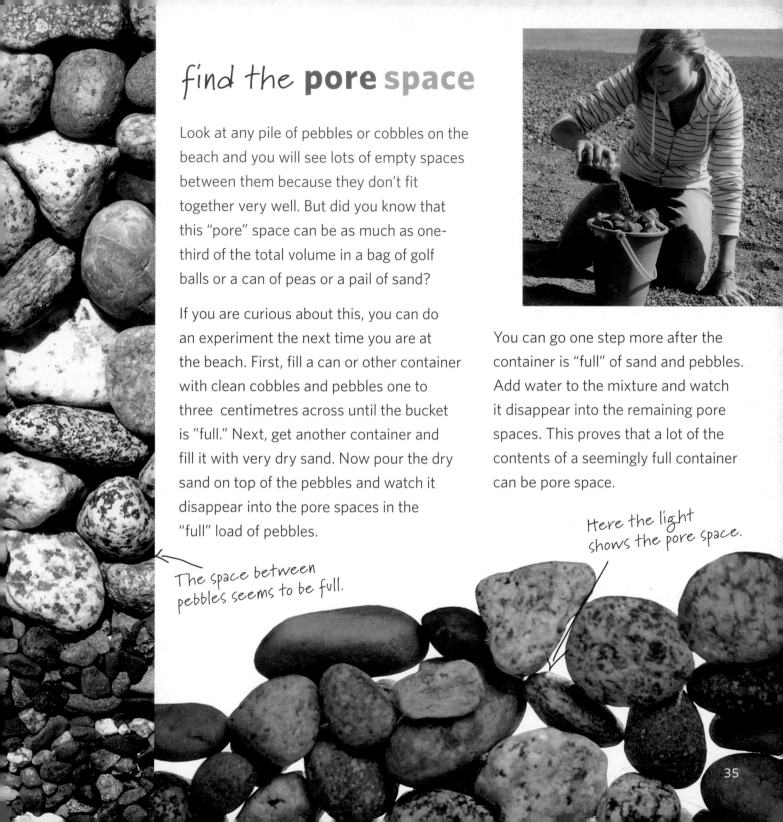

35

Sand grains brought up by ants from their tunnels tell of what's below

sand **points the way**

For prospectors, scientists and curious visitors, sands tell a good deal about the rocks in the area. For example, gold particles in sandbars point to gold-bearing rocks upstream. In northern Canada prospectors discovered that sand along some lakeshores contained grains of minerals usually found in diamond-bearing rocks. Later drilling through the frozen winter ice found what are now diamond mines. A Canadian geologist found a diamond deposit in Africa by drilling after finding that the sand in the surface ant hills contained the same indicator minerals.

musical sands!

Yes, there are musical sands! Swimmers and beach strollers are sometimes surprised by squeaking sounds as they walk along. It seems to happen only on special beaches where separation has concentrated special grains and less often on sand dunes. You may also have noticed that snow sometimes makes crisp, squeaking sounds on cold winter days as your footsteps compact it. But scientists are still puzzled about why sand squeaks. They have noticed, however, that squeaking sands seem be made of clean, smooth, well-rounded grains. One of the best beaches for this in Canada is near Souris, Prince Edward Island.

turtle tracks

On the Galapagos Islands female turtles crawl up to lay their eggs to hatch in the warm sand.

you need **damp sand** to make **castles**

Damp sand is not the same as dry sand to walk on, shovel or play with. This is because the water that makes the sand damp also acts as a weak glue. This leads to another idea – the angle of repose – the steepest you can pile a material without it slithering down and flattening out. If you experiment a little, you will find that dry sand sags into flat piles. On the other hand, you can make much steeper cones with damp sand, or even build sculptures such as castles and towers. You have probably also discovered that really soggy sand makes very flat piles. You can watch this happen when your steep pile of sand or castle gets flooded and flattened as the tide or waves come in.

angle of repose

Lake Ontario sand dune with wind ripples shows the angle of repose of dry sand, both on the dune and in the footprints

Sand sculpture, Parksville Beach Festival

37

6. collecting and identifying sand

You can use small bottles to collect samples of sand without making a mess. You can also look at the sand grains through the glass as you roll the bottle around in your hand. You should label your specimens and keep a record of where they come from. Very young scientists will want some sort of a sand pail with sloping sides to mould damp sand into castles and towers. A pail would also be useful for testing pore space.

Iron-rich magnetite grains in a black sand on a sheet of paper react to a round magnet underneath.

equipment for the adventuring sand scientist

You can add to your adventures in sand by taking a few things to the beach with you. A small, ordinary magnifying glass will help you see individual grains of sand more clearly. Sprinkle a few grains of sand on a sheet of paper and move a magnet under it. Use your magnifying glass to watch the black grains of magnetite, present in almost all beach sands, stand on end or follow the magnet as you move it.

Add a little sand and water to a pie plate or any shallow container with lipped edges and swish it round and round. Now watch the sand separate into different kinds with the dark minerals (including magnetite) being left behind as you swish the water around the edge. That is exactly the way panning for gold works.

how to identify sands

Hint number 1

If you have difficulty identifying sand grains on a beach because they are too small, look at the coarser pebbles and cobbles on the same beach because in most places, the finer sands are ground-up pieces of these same kinds of rock.

Hint number 2

When you arrive at a beach, look around to see if there are eroding banks or cliffs that are supplying the sand or gravel, and even boulders. That will often tell you something of what you should find in the sand.

Hint number 3

Colour is not entirely dependable as a way of identifying sands, but it is a useful place to begin. Look at the colours of the samples on the opposite page and pages 42-43 and start from there.

a Greenish sea urchin sand from Gros Morne National Park, Newfoundland.

b Shell sand with recognizable fragments, Florida.

c Yellow sand with coiled shell from Five Islands, Nova Scotia.

d Black volcanic sand, Buccaneer Island, Galapagos.

e Red, iron-stained sand, central Florida.

f White quartz sand, Copacabana, Rio de Janiero.

g Salt and pepper sand, Victoria, British Columbia.

h Green olivine sand, Eden Island, Galapagos.

i Light brown dune sand, Bartholomew Island, Galapagos.

In northern regions, **green sand** could be made of green urchin spines. In places of recent volcanic action, green sands are sometimes made of glassy green olivine crystals. Odd yellowish green sand grains may be made from rock stained with the mineral epidote.

Some **dark sands** come from the erosion of dark rocks such as ancient lavas or slates. You might have noticed that all sands look darker when wet. If you are in a volcanic region, the dark fragments are probably bits of lava. Black streaks on northern beaches are probably magnetite. A magnet will tell you right away.

Light rocks and shells produce light-coloured sand.

Coarse, dark sand with pebbles

"Salt and pepper" sand

Mixed sand of dark rock and pinkish granite

If the sand is white, it is probably either ground-up shells or quartz grains. If it is made of shells, you should be able to find some coarse, usually flattish grains that are clearly identifiable as parts of clam, snail, or coral shells. If the grains are very hard or irregular or round and glassy, they are probably quartz, the most common mineral by far in the world's beaches and dunes.

If the sand looks like "salt and pepper," it is a mixture of various kinds of materials. A great many Canadian sands are the "salt and pepper" type because they come from areas of granite that contain light-coloured quartz and feldspar and a few dark minerals such as magnetite and hornblende. Other salt and pepper sands come from erosion in areas of mixed rocks.

If the sand is pink or reddish, look around to see if nearby cliffs of reddish sandstone are being eroded. If the reddish colour occurs in streaks along a wave-washed beach and if the colour comes from glassy grains mixed with black magnetite, the red grains are usually red garnet. In parts of the world where red sea urchins are common, as in the Galapagos or British Columbia, small pockets of reddish sand may be made of ground-up red urchin spines.

If the sand is yellowish or pale brown, it is probably a shell sand lightly stained with iron oxide (rust) or a similarly stained quartz sand. The hardness of the grains will tell you which, because quartz grains are very much harder than shell grains. In fact, quartz will scratch glass.

Bits of glass bottles, pottery and brick quickly became part of this beach sand. Can you see them?

beware of **bricks** and **bottles**

Coquina or shell sand

Red pebbles from nearby glaciated red granite mean red sand nearby.

Humans are careless about throwing things away. When people throw glass bottles, bricks and chunks of cement into the sea, they get broken up and sneak into natural beach deposits. That's why you should be suspicious of the origin of reddish or yellowish brick-coloured pebbles and frosted and rounded bits of glass.

7. "new eyes" for sand

We live in a wonderful natural world. Endless diversity, mysteries, and beauty are to be found just by looking. You used to think of sand as the ordinary stuff we play with when we are very young or land on as we come in from surfing when we are older.

With your "new eyes" you know that beauty is to be found in its variety of grains, shapes, colours, and its transparency. There is adventure for our curious minds in uncovering the stories in sandstone cliffs and desert dunes, or squatting to look closely at the beach. Or even just walking in bare feet on rippled sands with waves breaking gently nearby.

It is even better to think that all this has been part of the landscape since solid Planet Earth first formed billions of years ago. The smell of the sea, the sound of the waves, the beauty in the sky and what's to be seen in the sand underfoot, are ever changing, ever beautiful.

Almost any square metre on a beach has stories to tell. Can you find ten stories in this beach picture?

For answers, see next page

*This book is dedicated
to the memory of our late
son, Christopher Ian Baird,
who left us much too soon.
His mother and I recall with
pleasure our family trips to
the beach together long ago.
There we shared the wonders
and the beauty to be found
in the workings of natural
laws, beginning in a simple
handful of sand.*

about the author

Geologist **DAVID McCURDY BAIRD** was born in Fredericton, New Brunswick and spent his early years in China with his missionary parents. After teaching geology in eastern Canadian universities, he became Founding Director of the National Museum of Science and Technology in Ottawa. He also created the Royal Tyrrell Museum in Alberta (the "Dinosaur Museum"). Dr. Baird has written a series of guides to the National Parks of Canada and contributed to numerous popular science programs for CBC-TV. Officer of the Order of Canada.

Copyright © 2009 David M. Baird

Library and Archives Canada Cataloguing in Publication

Baird, David M. (David McCurdy), 1920–
    Adventures in sand / by David M. Baird.

ISBN: 978-0-9812156-0-0

    1. Sand—Popular works. I. Title.

QE471.2.B33 2009   553.6'22   C2009-901509-9

The photograph of dinosaur tracks on page 27 is kindly supplied by the Royal Tyrrell Museum. All other photographs are by the author including the dinosaur on page 27 (permission from the Royal Tyrrell Museum) and the sand sculpture on page 37 (permission from the Parksville Beach Festival).

Design: Frances Hunter, Beacon Hill Communications Group Inc.

Printed in Canada by Friesens

Answers to question on page 45

1. white sand grains, probably quartz or shell fragments.
2. black sand, either magnetite or bits of dark rocks.
3. a few yellowish grains, especially lower left corner, (shells?).
4. wave currents have made separation patterns around pebbles and weeds.
5. at least five kinds of rock pebbles.
6. one large clam shell on its back.
7. clam shell has been partly filled with mostly light grains. even there, some separation of coloured grains.
8. bright green seaweed.
9. seaweed has bleached where it has dried.
10. one brownish fragment of wood or shell, lower left of centre.